Timothy Leary's
EIGHT CIRCUITS
OF THE BRAIN

edited by
Matthew Clark

Mahabongo Weeny Introductions
Vol. 4

1st Edition (2019)

Edited from a selection of works by Timothy Leary. Introduction by Matthew Clark.

ISBN: 9780992808891

Published by Psychedelic Press and Breaking Convention.
www.psychedelicpress.co.uk
www.breakingconvention.co.uk

Dr. Timothy Leary's work (©) has been republished with the kind permission of the Dr. Timothy Leary Futique Trust (administered by Zach Leary and Donna Scott), Michael Horowitz, Dr. Leary's Archivist (who specializes in rare and out-of-print books and papers on psychedelic science, literature, art and culture at ebay.ca/str/flashbackbookscanada), and Lisa Rein, Dr. Leary's Digital Librarian (timothylearyarchives.org).

Original cover image provided by Taylor Brearley. Graphic design and typesetting by HobGob Graphics.

For further information or to contact Matthew Clark, who provides lectures on the history, background, practice and philosophy of yoga and Indian religions:
e-mail: *matt@mahabongo.com*

Weeny Introductions

Vol. 1: *The Origins and Practices of Yoga: A Weeny Introduction (revised edition)*. Published by Lulu.com, 2018.

Vol. 2: *Sādhus, Sādhvīs, Nāgā Bābās: A Weeny Introduction* (two encyclopedia articles, limited to private circulation).

Vol. 3: *The History and Mythology of the Kumbh Melā*. Published by Lulu.com, 2018.

Vol. 4: *The Eight Circuits of the Brain*, by Timothy Leary, edited by Matthew Clark. Published by Psychedelic Press and Breaking Convention, 2019.

Vol. 5: *A Drop of Rain in Asia: A Brief Introduction to Traditional Burmese Medicine*, by Dr. U Win Ko, edited by John Hamwee and Matthew Clark. Published by Lulu.com, 2013.

Also by Matthew Clark

The Daśnāmī-Saṃnyāsīs: The Integration of Ascetic Lineages into an Order. Leiden/Boston. E. J. Brill, 2006.

The Tawny One: Soma, Haoma and Ayahuasca. London/New York: Muswell Hill Press, 2017.

Music (pop/jazz) by Matthew Clark (Mahabongo)

Swish It's Everywhere (2006)
Minus Ridiculous (2012)
Murmuration (2015)
The Banyan Tree (2016)
Starfish Five (2019)

Contents

Contents

Introduction

D r. Timothy Leary (1920–1996) wrote or co-wrote over thirty books and contributed hundreds of essays, interviews and articles to journals and magazines: on psychology, consciousness, psychedelic drugs, cyber-culture, politics and other issues. Leary's 'post-enlightenment' publications (from 1960 onwards) were, in general, part-autobiographical and part-'new psychology'. The books that he wrote in the 1970s are, I believe, particularly interesting, as they elaborate on his eight circuit theory of the brain.

According to Leary's account in *What Does WoMan Want,*[1] the ideas for the theory were originally inspired after studying a set of twenty-four images on parchment, like picture postcards, that had been acquired in Bengal from a guru called Siva-ji by Professor Adams, a scholar of Hinduism and Buddhism in the Oriental Philosophy Department of Rutger's University. The twenty-four images on parchment are said to resemble Tarot pictues, with twelve images representing past human development, and twelve representing future human evolution. The two sets of twelve images were explained by Adams to be representative of the twelve signs of the astrological zodiac, the I Ching, and the twelve divinities of the Greek and Roman pantheon.

Adams had become interested in yoga, which he practised regularly, and when on sabbatical leave in 1961 went to Bengal, studied Tantra for nine months with Siva-ji and acquired the name Aryabhata. Adams eventually returned to America, left his wife and children, legally acquired a hundred hits of LSD and began experimenting with LSD and Tantric sex in the Virgin Islands with a younger partner, Sylvia. After experiences of cosmic sexual union, Adams and Sylvia returned to New York and for a while led a partially 'normal' life. However, they went back to Calcutta,

---

1. The story is scattered in several parts throughout the book, beginning on p. 137ff.

where Siva-ji gave Adams the parchment manuscript, said to be between two and seven hundred years old, and told him to take it to Leary. Adams then brought the parchment in October 1963 to Leary at the Millbrook estate in upstate New York, where Leary lived from 1963 to 1967.

It is hard to know how accurate the account of the parchment is, as *What Does WoMan Want* is partly fictionalised. Furthermore, there is another account in *The Fugitive Philosopher*.[2] Someone called Prince Alexis shows Leary, when he is in Switzerland after his escape from prison in the USA, a set of twenty-four pictures of astrologically-based evolution contained in a leather-bound manuscript from Nepal.

One of these stories may be true (or otherwise), but Leary's original scheme, as presented in *Neurologic* (1973), was of seven circuits, and in that scheme there are no occult correspondences or mention of twenty-four stages of evolution, as supposedly represented in the manuscript and in later versions of the theory, which have eight circuits.[3] It seems probable that Leary's original scheme was based on the seven *cakra* [chakra] system that features in some Hindu and Buddhist *Tantra*s.[4]

Leary's circuits theory of the brain/nervous system was mostly developed between 1973 and 1976 while he was in prison, from where the text for *Neurologic* was smuggled out on scraps of paper. Although the theory appeared in several subsequent publications, the fullest treatments are in *Exo-Psychology* (1977)[5] and *The Game of Life* (1979).

Inherent in the later and more fully developed model[6] of the eight-circuits are 'octave' correspondences, which of course applies directly to music (which Leary

---

2. (Compiled by Beverly R. Potter.) Berkeley: Ronin Publishing, Inc., 2007, pp. 139–55.

3. See *Neurologic* by Joanna and Timothy Leary (San Francisco: Starseed Information Centre, 1973). The details of the scheme are almost the same as in later publications but circuits seven and eight (of the later theory) are largely combined.

4. The scheme of seven *cakra*s was initially popularized in the West by the publication in 1915 of the *Principles of Tantra* and a translation of the *Mahānirvāṇa Tantra* by Arthur Avalon/John Woodroffe. Although the scheme of six-plus-one (or seven) *cakra*s is to be found in Tantric texts, there are also schemes in *Tantra*s of four, five, six and nine *cakra*s.

5. Republished as *Info-Psychology* (Tempe, Arizona: New Falcon Publishing, 1989).

6. Later publications contain an eight-circuit scheme and, in most versions, occult correspondences. The eight-circuit scheme appears in *What Does WoMan Want* (Dexter, Oregon: 88 Books, 1976), and in detail in *Exo-Psychology* (Culver City: Starseed/Peace Press, 1977), *Neuropolitics* (co-authored with Robert Anton Wilson and George A. Koopman. Los Angeles: Starseed/Peace Press, 1977), and *The Game of Life* (Culver City, California: Starseed/Peace Press, 1979). The scheme is also presented (more briefly) in *The Intelligence Agents* (Culver City: Peace Press, Inc., 1979, pp. 92–95), *Neuropolitique* (Las Vegas: Falcon Press, 1988, pp. 87–115), *Design For Dying*, co-authored with R. U. Sirius (London: Thorsons, 1997, pp. 83–91), and in Robert Anton Wilson's *Cosmic Trigger: The Final Secret of the Illuminati* (Berkeley, California: And/Or Press, 1977, pp. 197–209), which is a slightly edited version of the text of *Neuropolitics*, pp. 84–93. The scheme also features in a comic entitled *NeuroComics*, by Timothy Leary, Pete von Sholly, and George Di Caprio (San Francisco: Last Gasp Eco-Funnies, 1979), which was translated into German (trans. Gregor Pott): *Neurocomic* (Basel: Sphinx Verlag, 1981). Another publication in German, *Neurologic* (Der Grüne Zweig, 39, trans. Dietmar Höhne). Löhrbach: Werner Pieper's MedienXperimente/ ReEducation, n.d.) is based on Leary's seven-circuit model, as it appears in *Neurologic*. An introduction by Leary to the eight-circuit theory, edited from *Exo-Psychology*, can also be found in *Metaphors of Consciousness*, edited by Ronald S. Valle and Rolf von Eckartsberg (New York/London: Plenum Press, pp. 179–197).

does not mention), but which are extended to traditional occult systems: the I Ching, Tarot, astrology, the Hebrew alphabet and classical Greco-Roman mythology. Implicit in these associations is the idea that there is neat structure in the universe that applies to various forms of thought and which governs the entire course of biological and human evolution.

However, as R. U. Sirius comments: "During his later years he didn't talk much about it. I think as he embraced 'chaos', he wanted to distance himself from the tidiness of the model".[7] One of Leary's main motifs from the mid-seventies onwards was S.M.I.^{2}L.E. (Space Migration, Intelligence Increase, Life Extension), concepts that were embodied in his eight-circuit model of the brain.[8] Although from a scientific perspective the model is as 'out-there' as it gets, it nevertheless provides a refreshingly different perspective on where we might have come from and on where we might be going; and any theory on such matters is surely to be welcomed. Besides Leary's model, there is practically no other theory of evolution, as far as I am aware, that attempts to account for many of the peculiarities of human development in terms of the amazing course of technological innovation.[9]

While nearly all of the text in this booklet is in Leary's own words, from two books in particular,[10] it has occasionally been slightly edited and reorganized; some paragraphs have been moved to footnotes, and also I have added several introductory

---

7. *Design For Dying*, p. 91.

8. As noted in a footnote above, and by John Higgs (*I Have America Surrounded: The Life of Timothy Leary*. London: Friday Books, 2006, p. 252), the eight-fold model evolved from Leary's previous seven-fold models, versions of which were presented in *The Politics of Ecstasy* (as the 'Seven Tongues of God', or the 'Seven Basic Spiritual Questions') and other publications at the end of the 1960s. In the 'Berkeley Lectures' of 1969 (see *The Delicious Grace of Moving One's Hand: The Collected Sex Writings*. New York: Thunder's Mouth Press, 1998, pp. 160–172) Leary outlines seven levels of consciousness, which has some similarities with his eight-fold model. However, in the later model, Asian religious notions and God are replaced by DNA consciousness and other 'scientific' concepts. Interestingly, an eight-fold scheme reappears in *Your Brain Is God* (Berkeley: Ronin Publishing, 1988, pp. 14–18) as 'The Eight Crafts of God', which are framed as eight metaphysical questions about existence; but in this publication there is no mention of the eight circuits of the brain or of the occult.

9. The ideas of the eight-circuit brain are the main basis of Robert Anton Wilson's *Prometheus Rising* (Grand Junction, Colorado: Hilaritas Press, 2016 (2nd edn.) [1983]), and also feature in several of his other publication, including: *Quantum Psychology: How Brain Software Programs You and Your World* (Tempe, Arizona: New Falcon Publications, 1992); *Reality is What You Can Get Away with* (New York: Dell Publishing Company, 1995); *The Illuminati Papers* (Oakland, California: Ronin Publishers Inc., 1997 [1980]); and the *Schrödinger's Cat Trilogy* (New York: Bantam Doubleday/ Dell Publishing Group, 1998). However, Wilson names the circuits slightly differently and in *Prometheus Rising* and *Quantum Psychology* Circuits 6 and 7 are transposed from the way they are in Leary's scheme (as Circuits 7 and 6). For an explanation of why Wilson changes the order of these circuits, see *Prometheus Rising* (2016:281–290).

　　Antero Alli developed a map of consciousness and personal development based on Leary's eight-circuit model (*Angel Tech: A Modern Shaman's Guide to Reality Selection* (Santa Monica, California: [Vigilantero Press/Falcon Press]/New Falcon Publications, [1985/1986]/1991); more recently elaborated in *The Eight-Circuit Brain: Navigational Strategies for the Energetic Body.* (Tempe, Arizona: The Original Falcon Press, 2014 [2009]). In a similar line, Laurent Huguelit also explores personal development and the eight-circuit brain in *The Shamanic Path to Quantum Consciousness: The Eight Circuits of Creative Power* (trans. Jack Cain. Rochester, Vermont/Toronto: Bear & Company, 2014). Leary only occasionally makes correspondences between terrestrial and post-terrestrial circuits (1 and 5, 2 and 6, 3 and 7, 4 and 8); however, this idea is significantly elaborated by Wilson, Alli and Huguelit.

10. The main scheme is taken from *The Game of Life*, pp. 49–59, while the explanations for each main circuit are from *Neuropolitics*, pp. 84–93. A few explanatory comments from his other publications have also been inserted.

paragraphs and explanatory footnotes of my own. Although the scheme of the eight-circuit model of the brain and the text of this booklet have been available for many years in several of Leary's publications and on the internet I thought it might be useful to collate all the information in a handy form. It is now nearly fifty years since Leary's writings on this theory were smuggled out of Folsom prison, where Leary was incarcerated. Regardless of the plausiblity or otherwise of his theory, I believe that it has an intrinsic historical interest; it merits being republished.

This short book was written ten years ago but only recently I decided to publish it. Many thanks to James Penner, Denis Berry, Lisa Rein and Michael Horowitz for making connections, to Michael Horowitz for his helpful comments on earlier drafts, and to Donna Scott and Zach Leary, who administer Timothy Leary's estate, all of whom helped facilitate publication. Many thanks also to Rob Dickins and all at Psychedelic Press and Breaking Convention for publishing this volume.

Matthew Clark (editor), Hove, England (June, 2019)

The eight circuits of the brain/nervous-system

Working with the theory of Francis Crick that life (DNA) may have been seeded on Earth ('Directed Panspermia'),[11] Leary presents the scheme below of twenty-four stages of evolution of DNA. The Earth is believed to be one of many millions of planets inhabited by life. Planets are periodically seeded by bio-genetic intelligence. Once seeded, DNA evolves according to a pre-determined sequence, eventually allowing life to decode itself and develop the technology to transport itself, via H.O.M.E.s (High-Orbital Mini-Earths: see below) space-ships, and by other (currently) science-fiction means, to other womb planets, where the process may begin again. According to Leary, there are eight circuits of the brain/nervous-system, four of which are terrestrial, and four of which are extra- (or post-) terrestrial. The terrestrial circuits are said to operate primarily in the left hemisphere of the brain, while the post-terrestrial circuits primarily operate in the right hemisphere of the brain.[12] Leary occasionally referred to the post-terrestrial circuits as being, respectively, in the domains of the body (Circuit 5), brain (Circuit 6), DNA (Circuit 7) and the quantum structure (Circuit 8); progressively smaller areas contolling larger spacial regions.

Each of the eight circuits has three phases or stages, making twenty-four circuits in total. The three phases (or functions) are based on the structure of the synapse.[13] The scheme of the eight-circuit brain is also said to have corresponding representations in all of the world's major occult systems, the correspondences to

---

11. Leary concludes (*Game Of Life*, p. 61) that, "it is possible that life reached earth in this way, but that scientific evidence is inadequate at this present time to say anything about the probability."

12. The theory of the two hemispheres of the brain (right and left) having intrinsically different functions was first popularized by Robert E. Ornstein (*The Psychology of Consciousness*. San Francisco: W. H. Freeman and Co., 1972). According to the theory, the right hemisphere of the brain governs the left side of the body, and is associated with pattern recognition, 'holistic mentations', our orientation in space, artistic endeavour, crafts, body image and recognition of faces. The left hemisphere, governing the right side of the body, is predominantly involved with analytical, logical thinking, especially in verbal and mathematical functions. Its mode of operation is primarily 'linear', as information is processed sequentially. Julian Jaynes' *The Origin of Consciousness in the Breakdown of the Bicameral Mind* (Boston: Houghton Mifflin Company, 1976) is another popular and fascinating exporation of the roles of brain hemispheres in culture and consciousness. The models of both Ornstein and Jaynes model have been challenged by several scientists. However, more recently, a more sophisticated account of the functions of the two hemisperes of the brain has been cogently articulated by the neuroscientist Iain McGilchrist in *The Master and his Emissary: The Divided Brain and the Making of the Western World* (New Haven/London: Yale University Press, 2010).

13. The receptor first receives a signal; the nucleus then integrates the signal; and the effector then transmits the signal outward to whatever nerves, glands or muscles may be appropriate.

6

which are schematically presented in the pages that follow.[14] However, the scheme of the eight circuits of consciousness may be understood without taking into account any of the occult correspondences, which are included merely for their intrinsic interest.

When life has evolved through twelve embryonic stages (the four terrestrial circuits of the brain), it leaves the womb-planet and assumes self-actualized existence in the galaxy, fabricating H.O.M.E.s. The unit of life is the gene-pool. In advanced species—social insects, 'humants'—the genetic unit is the hive. The key factor of evolution is the formation of the new hives by the fusion of self-actualized winged elite out-castes, who migrate from the old hive into a new ecological niche.

---

14. I surmise that the occult correspondences may have been substantially informed by Robert Anton Wilson; they sometimes seem quite tenuous. Further information on this aspect of the system is presented in *The Game of Life*.

Explanation of the eight circuits of the brain
by Timothy Leary

Nearly all of the text that follows is in Leary's own words, which are from the publications noted in the editor's introduction

Overview of the eight circuits

(Terrestrial circuits)

Circuit 1	Bio-survival (fight/flee), 'marine' intelligence
Circuit 2	Emotional-mammalian, 'terratorial' intelligence
Circuit 3	Linguistic, artefact, tool-making intelligence
Circuit 4	Social, hierarchical, 'hive' intelligence

(Post-terrestrial circuits)

Circuit 5	Hedonistic, 'hive-free' intelligence
Circuit 6	Cyber, electronic, reality-creation intelligence
Circuit 7	Creating life, physical immortality, DNA intelligence
Circuit 8	Neuro-atomic, post-biological intelligence

The progression through the eight circuits of the brain, each of which is serially activated, is a process that determines the evolution of the human species. The general process of evolution is mirrored in the growth and development of the child, who in the process of 'growing up' will sequentially pass through all the previous stages of general biological evolution. The nervous system 'meta-morphizes' through the twenty-four stages in eight ecological niches: 1. in water; 2. on land; 3. in artefact shelters (tribal); 4. in cities (insectoid); 5. in 'hedonests' fabricated by self-actualized bodies; 6. in H.O.M.E.s fabricated by self-controlled brains; 7. in fabricated DNA hives; 8. in quantum-gravitational fields.

When brain-circuits are sequentially activated, the person/organism passes through the specific experiences and activities associated with each of these circuits. The more evolved the human culture is, the greater the number of circuits that will have been activated. So-called 'primitive' cultures will have only activated the lower circuits of the brain.[15]

---

15. Another feature of the process is the notion that, historically, consciousness has evolved (and the species has

The imprinting of the first three of the eight circuits determines, by about the age of three-and-a-half, the basic degree and style of trust/distrust that will colour consciousness, the degree and style of assertiveness/submissiveness that will determine 'ego' status, and the degree of cleverness/clumsiness with which the 'mind' will handle tools or ideas. In evolutionary terms, the first-brain 'consciousness' is basically invertebrate, passively floating towards nurture, and retreating from danger. Second-brain 'ego' is mammalian, always struggling for status in the tribal pecking order. Third-brain 'mind' is hominid, hooked into human culture and dealing with life through a matrix of human-made gadgets and human-created symbolism. The fourth brain is post-hominid, specifically characteristic of homo sapiens, the domesticated WoMan.

These four circuits are normally the only networks of the brain that are activated. It should become clear why they are called terrestrial. They have evolved on, and have been shaped by the gravitational, climatic, and energy conditions determining survival and reproduction on this kind of planet circling this variety of Type G star. Intelligent organisms evolving in space, not living at the bottom of a 4,000-mile gravity well, not competing for territory on a finite planet-surface, not limited by the forward-back, up-down, left-right parameters of earthly life, would inevitably develop different circuits, which are imprinted differently, and not so inflexibly Euclidean.[16]

It is no accident, then, that our logic (and our computer-design) follows the either/or, binary structure of these circuits. Nor is it an accident that our geometry, until the twentieth century, has been Euclidean. Euclid's geometry, Aristotle's logic and Newton's physics are meta-programs, which synthesize and generalize first-circuit/brain 'forward-back', second-circuit/brain 'up-down', and third-circuit/brain 'right-left' programs. The fourth circuit/brain, which deals with the transmission of tribal or ethnic culture across generations, introduces the fourth dimension: time, which binds cultures.

---

evolved) in an east to west direction, from the ancient world of the east, through Greece, Rome, medieval Europe, and on to America; California is, of course, the 'new frontier', the 'sun-belt' of more 'switched-on' brains. Higgs (*I Have America Surrounded*, p. 250) comments that, "This was not one of his more convincing ideas, as anyone with a basic grasp of Chinese or Islamic history would be the first to point out, but it did highlight a new patriotism that appears in his writings after the last vestiges of the Nixon administration crumbled away" [editor's footnote].

16. *Forward-back*: is the basic binary choice programmed by the bio-computer operating on Circuit 1: either advance, go forward, sniff it, touch it, taste it, bite it; or retreat, back away, flee, escape. *Up-down*: is the basic gravitational sense; it appears in all ethological reports of animal combat: rear up, swell the body to maximum size, growl, howl, shriek; or cringe, drop the tail between the legs, murmur softly, skulk away, crawl and shrink the body size. These are domination and submission signals common to the iguana, dog, bird, and Chairman of the Board of the local bank. These reflexes make up Circuit 2 'ego'. *Left-right*: is basic to the polarity of body-design on the planetface. Right-hand dominance, and the associated preference for the linear left-lobe functions of the brain, determine our normal modes of artefact-manufacture and conceptual thought, i.e. Circuit 3 'mind'. Asymmetry is the key to improved brain-function.

Since each of these circuits consists of bio-chemical imprints or matrices in the nervous system, each of them is specifically triggered by neuro-transmitter, i.e. drugs. ('Activation' of a brain/circuit most probably results from a general suppression of higher neural circuits, which leaves a particular brain dominant.) The terrestrial drugs that activate particular circuits (see below) do not change basic bio-chemical imprints. The behaviours that they trigger are those that were wired into the nervous system during the first stages of imprint vulnerability (the Circuit 2 drunk exhibits the emotional games or cons learned from parents in infancy; the Circuit 3 'mind' never gets beyond the permutations and combinations of those artefacts and symbols originally imprinted, or abstractions associated with the imprints through later conditioning; and so forth).

TERRESTRIAL CIRCUITS

CIRCUIT 1: Biosurvival Circuit: Mastery of Marine Neuro-Technology
In species: unicellular.
In individual: viscerotonic-endomorphic (infancy).
Ecological niche: water.
Reality goal: safety

Stage 1   passive-receptive; bio-survival; first childhood; sucking-floating
technology; amoeboid intelligence
Zodiac: Pisces I   *Tarot*: Fool
I Ching: Kun (Earth)
Hebrew: Aleph ('I am undefined, undirected')
Roman: Pluto-Proserpine
Greek: Hades-Persephone

Stage 2   bio-survival intelligence; bio-survival brain; the first self-
actualization; biting-squirming technology; fish intelligence;
discovery that the external world can be controlled by crying
Zodiac: Aries I   *Tarot*: Magician
I Ching: Kun (Earth)
Hebrew: Beth ('a young man will take heed')
Roman: Neptune, Amphitrite
Greek: Poseidon, Amphitrite

Stage 3   active-external bio-survival fusion; the first migration; crawling
technology; amphibian intelligence; oxygen-snorting amphibian
crawls onto the earth
Zodiac: Taurus I   *Tarot*: (Earth) Empress
I Ching: Kun (Earth)
Hebrew: Gimel ('deal bountifully with me that I may live')
Roman: Demeter-Bacchus
Greek: Ceres-Dionysus

This marine or vegetative brain was the first to evolve (a billion years ago) and is the first brain to be activated at birth. It programs perception onto an either/or grid, which is divided into nurturing-helpful 'things' (which it approaches) and noxious-dangerous 'things' (which it flees from or attacks). The imprinting of this circuit sets up the basic attitude of trust or suspicion, which will last for life. It also identifies the external stimuli that will ever after trigger approach or avoidance.

In popular speech, the first brain is generally called 'consciousness' per se: the sense of being biologically alive, in 'this' body, orientated to the survival of the body. (When you are 'unconscious', the first circuit is anaesthetized and doctors may perform surgery on you, or enemies may attack you, and you will not evade them or flee.)

To activate the first circuit/brain, take an opiate, which will bring you down to cellular intelligence, bio-survival passivity, to the floating consciousness of the newborn. (This is why Freudians identify opiate addiction with the desire to return to infancy.)

CIRCUIT 2: **Emotional (Locomotional) Circuit:**
Mastery of Mammalian Technology
In species: mammalian musculotonic-mesomorphic
In individual: early childhood
Ecological niche: land
Reality goal: herd security

Stage 4
emotional; passive-receptive; power by evasion; sensory acuteness and camouflage; second childhood; running technology; small animal intelligence (rabbits, rodents, weasels, lawyers)
Zodiac: Gemini I   *Tarot*: (Sly) Priestess
I Ching: Ch'en (Movement)
Hebrew: Da Leth ('remove me from the way of lying')
Roman: Mercury   *Greek*: Hermes

Stage 5
emotional-muscular power intelligence; the second self-actualization; territorial control technology; large animal intelligence (lions, tigers, bears, low-level politicians); one/two-year-old territorial brat; personal reality claimed and possessed ('my mother', 'my room', 'my toys')
Zodiac: Cancer I   *Tarot*: Emperor
I Ching: Ch'en (Movement)
Hebrew: He ('I shall keep it until the end')
Roman: Vesta, Lares-Penates   *Greek*: Hestia

Stage 6
(emotional) active-externalization of power; the second migration; social communication technology; monkey-gestural intelligence; formation of second hive (monkey-troop); three/four-year-old show-off; beginning of communication links outside the family; survival not through strength but social communication and tree-top altitude allowing overview
Zodiac: Leo I   *Tarot*: Pope
I Ching: Ch'en (Movement)
Hebrew: Vau ('my hands I will lift up to your laws')
Roman: Apollo, Antiope   *Greek*: Apollo, Hyppolyta

This second, more advanced bio-computer emerged when vertebrates appeared and began to compete for territory (perhaps 500,000,000 BC). In the individual, it is activated when the DNA master-tape triggers the metamorphosis from crawling to walking. As every parent knows, the toddler is no longer a passive (bio-vegetative) infant but a mammalian politician, full of physical (and emotional) territorial demands, quick to meddle in family business and decision-making. Again, the first imprint on this circuit remains constant for life (unless brain-washed) and identifies the stimuli that automatically trigger dominant, aggressive behaviour or submissive, cooperative behaviour. When we say that a person is behaving emotionally, egotistically or 'like a two-year-old', we say that SHe is blindly following one of the robot imprints on this circuit.

The second circuit, in vernacular language, is called 'ego'. The so-called 'ego' is the second-circuit, mammalian sense of status (importance/unimportance) in the pack or tribe.

To activate the second circuit/brain, take an abundant quantity of alcohol. Vertebrate territorial patterns and mammalian emotions immediately appear when the booze flows, as Thomas Nashe intuitively realized when he characterized the various alcohol states by animal labels: 'ass drunk', 'goat drunk', 'swine drunk', 'bear drunk' etc.

CIRCUIT 3: Laryngeal-Manipulation/Mental
Symbolic/Dexterity-Symbolism Circuit:
Using Neuro-Technology To Manufacture Your Environment
In species: ectomorphic pre-civilized human
In individual: cerebrotonic (pre-adolescent childhood)
Ecological niche: man-made symbolic-artefact
Reality goal: hive sanity

Stage 7   passive acceptance of artefacts (caves, stones and hive-
symbols); receptive mind; mimetic; repetitive use of symbols;
third childhood; self-definition; passive consumer of laryngeal-
manual technology; Palaeolithic intelligence
Zodiac: Virgo I   *Tarot*: Lovers
I Ching: Kan (Water/Toil)
Hebrew: Zain ('your word has quickened me')
Roman: Diana-Narcissus   *Greek*: Artemis-Hyacinthus

Stage 8   laryngeal intelligence; invention of symbols and using
tools; the third self-actualization; Neolithic-creative
intelligence; six- to eight-year-olds;
Zodiac: Libra I   *Tarot*: Chariot Driver
I Ching: Kan (Water/Toil)
Hebrew: Cheth ('I thought on my ways')
Roman: Prometheus
Greek: Prometheus-Psyche, Mnemosyne

Stage 9   active-external cooperative manipulation of symbols;
formation of third Hive (the tribe); the third migration (to
technological trading centres); division of labour
technology; tribal intelligence; invention of money as a
means of exchange and collaboration; twelve-year-olds;
joining Scouts or armed forces
Zodiac: Scorpio I   *Tarot*: Strength
I Ching: Kan (Water/Toil)
Hebrew: Teth ('your teaching is better than gold or silver')
Roman: Minerva, Theseus
Greek: Athena, Vulcan

This third circuit/brain emerged when hominid types began to differentiate from other primate stock (*c.* 4–5 million BC), and is activated when the older child begins handling artefacts and sending/receiving laryngeal signals (human speech units). The child learns about representing basic realities through language, writing, speaking and signifying. If the environment is stimulating to the third circuit, the child takes a 'bright' imprint and becomes dextrous and articulate; if the environment is inhabited by deliberately stupid people, the child takes a 'dumb' imprint, i.e. remains more or less at a five-year-old stage of symbol-blindness.

The third circuit is what we generally call 'mind': the capacity to receive, integrate and transmit signals produced by the hominid hand (artefacts) or the hominid laryngeal muscles (speech). Up until recent generations, the vast majority of humans never moved beyond this stage.

To activate the third circuit/brain, try coffee or tea, a high-protein diet, speed or cocaine.

CIRCUIT 4: **(Sexual) Domestication Circuit (Hive Socialization): Using Culture As Neuro-Technology To Form Human-Urban Hives**
Ecological niche: monotheistic-hive structures (cities)
Reality goal: selection and maintenance of approved hive socio-sex role

Stage 10
self-indulgent monarchical stage; sexual impersonation; fourth childhood; king and aristocracy as self-indulgent patrons of new technologies; adolescence; monotheism as device for organizing tribes into centralized poly-caste hives
Zodiac: Sagittarius I   *Tarot*: Hermit
I Ching: Ken (Protection)
Hebrew: Yod ('you have afflicted me with faithfulness')
Roman: Mars-Venus
Greek: Ares-Aphrodite

Stage 11
familialization; the fourth self-actualization; family orientated; democratic civilization; domestic intelligence; home-owner; sexuality harnessed to domestic responsibility; Protestant/capitalist/democratic society 1559–1859
Zodiac: Capricorn I   *Tarot*: Wheel of Life
I Ching: Ken (Protection)
Hebrew: Kaph ('I am like a bottle in the smoke')
Roman: Juno-Jupiter
Greek: Hera-Zeus

Stage 12
egalitarian homogenization; formation of fourth hive; centralized insectoid-monotheistic state; the fourth migration; Maoist anthill socialism/welfare-state religious society 1859–1976; terror of aging and death
Zodiac: Aquarius I   *Tarot*: Justice
I Ching: Ken (Protection)
Hebrew: Lamed ('they continue this day according to your ordinances, for all are your servants')
Roman: the Caesar principle
Greek: Themis, Nemesis, Aidos

This fourth circuit/brain was formed when hominid packs evolved into societies and programmed specific sex-roles for their members, c. 30,000 BC. In the individual it is activated at puberty, when the DNA triggers glandular release of sexual neurochemicals, and the metamorphosis to adulthood begins. The first orgasms or mating experiences imprint a characteristic sex-role, which, again, is bio-chemically bonded and remains constant for life, unless some form of brainwashing or chemical re-imprinting is accomplished.[17]

In daily speech, fourth-circuit imprints and programs are known as the 'adult personality', the domesticated sexual impersonation.

The specific neuro-transmitter for the fourth circuit/brain has not yet been synthesized, but it is generated by the glands after pubescence and flows volcanically through the blood streams of adolescents. The 'socialization' drugs are sedatives, Prozac and television.

---

17. Masters and Johnson have demonstrated that specific sexual 'dysfunctions'—so-called 'perversions', 'fetishes', low- or no-performance conditions like premature ejaculation, impotence, frigidity, etc., or eccentric inputs defined as 'sinful' by the local tribe—are determined by specific experiences in early adolescent mating. The same is true for the equally robotic behaviour of the 'normal', 'well-adjusted' person. The sex-role (or, as it might more appropriately be called, the 'sexual impersonation style'), of the human is as rote and repetitious as that of any other mammal (or bird or fish or insect).

POST-TERRESTRIAL CIRCUITS

The Pavlovian-Skinnerian robotism of the first four circuits changes drastically and dramatically when we turn to the right-lobe, the future circuits and extra-terrestrial chemicals. The four evolving future 'brains' are:

CIRCUIT 5: Neurosomatic Circuit (Culture-Free, Hive-Free, Gravity-Free, Hedonic): Escaping Insectoid Hives Using Automobile Body
Ecological niche (in individual): one's own body
Ecological niche (in species): zones of high technology and affluence in Stage 12 empires
Reality goal: control of one's own body; somatic self-reward

Stage 13   neurosomatic receptivity; self-definition as pleasure elite; self-indulgence; hedonic consumption; sensual awareness of the body; fifth childhood; post-hive body consciousness; zero-gravity liberation; the 'hippy'
Zodiac: Pisces II   *Tarot*: Hanging Man
I Ching: Tui (Pleasure/Joyous Lake)
Hebrew: Mem
('I have refrained my feet from the evil way of earth')
Titan: Tethys

Stage 14   neurosomatic intelligence; the body-mind; fifth self-actualization; body control; somatic self reward; executive management of body as time-ship; the 'yogin'; post-hive disciplined control of the body; control of one's own aesthetic environment and responses
Zodiac: Aries II   *Tarot*: Horse (or Death)
I Ching: Tui (Pleasure/Joyous Lake)
Hebrew: Nun ('your word is a lamp unto my feet')
Titan: Oceanus

Stage 15   neurosomatic fusion; the 'new body' of fused adepts; Tantric linkage of self-actualized bodies; escape from your own body via neurosomatic fusion; creation of neurosomatic diploid bi-person having homologous, paired brain-circuits for each stage; formation of fifth hive; intentional communes;[18] the fifth migration; fusion of winged, hedonic elites; fusion of self-fabricated realities

Zodiac: Taurus II   *Tarot*: Temperance
I Ching: Tui (Pleasure/Joyous Lake)
Hebrew: Sameck ('you hold me up and I shall be safe')
Titan: Rhea

When this fifth 'body-brain' is activated, flat Euclidean figure-ground configurations explode multi-dimensionally. Gestalts shift, in McLuhan's terms, from linear visual space to all-encompassing sensory space. A hedonic turn-on occurs, a rapturous amusement, a detachment from the previously compulsive mechanism of the first four circuits; a transcendence of 'guilty' domestic circuits. The fifth brain began to appear about 4,000 years ago in the first leisure-class civilizations, and has been increasing statistically in recent centuries (even before the Drug Revolution), a fact demonstrated by the hedonic art of India, China, Rome and other affluent societies. More recently, Ornstein and his school have demonstrated with electro-encephalograms that this circuit represents the first jump from the linear left-lobe of the brain to the analogical right-lobe. The opening and imprinting of this circuit has been the preoccupation of 'technicians of the occult', of Tantric shamans and hatha-yogis. While the fifth-circuit imprint can be achieved through sensory deprivation, social isolation, physiological stress or severe shock (through ceremonial terror tactics, as practised by such rascal-gurus as Don Juan, Matus or Aleister Crowley), it has traditionally been reserved for the educated aristocracy of leisure societies which have solved the four terrestrial survival problems.

It is no accident that the pot-head generally refers to hir neural state as 'high' or 'spaced-out'. The transcendence of gravitational, digital, linear, either-or, Aristotelian, Newtonian, Euclidean, planetary orientations (Circuits 1–4) is, in evolutionary perspective, part of our neurological preparation for the inevitable migration off the home planet, which is now beginning. (This is why so many pot-heads are Star Trek freaks and Sci-Fi adepts.) The extra-terrestrial meaning of being

---

18. On the downside: wacky cosmic cults.

'high' is confirmed by astronauts themselves. Most of those who have entered the free-fall of zero gravity describe 'mystic experiences' or rapture states typical of the neurosomatic circuit.[19] Free-fall, at the proper evolutionary time, triggers the neurosomatic mutation, previously achieved through yogic training or the fifth-circuit stimulant, cannabis. (MDA/X.T.C and low-dose psychedelics also trigger this circuit.) Surfing, skiing, sky-diving and the new sexual culture (sensuous massage, vibrators, imported Tantric arts, etc.) have evolved at the same time as part of the hedonic conquest of gravity. The 'turned-on' state is always described as 'floating', or, in the Zen metaphor, 'one foot above the ground'.

---

19. "No photo can show how beautiful the earth looked", raves Captain Ed Mitchell, describing his illumination in free-fall. He sounds like any successful yogi or pot-head. No camera can show this experience because it is inside the nervous system. Captain Mitchell has left Aero Space to found the Institute of Noetic Sciences, concerned with scientific research into right-lobe functions. Buzz Aldrin has joined him.

CIRCUIT 6: Neuro-Electric/Neurophysical/Cyber-Electronic
Circuit (Einsteinian): Using Your Own Brain To Fabricate
New Realities
Ecological niche (in individual): brain
Ecological niche (in species): in far-western affluent-elite
technological frontiers
Reality goal: control of one's own brain; neurological
self-reward

Stage 16   neuro-electric passive-receptive; self-indulgence; self-definition
as neurological organism; passive awareness of the vibratory
nature of reality; reality relativism; watching your own brain
fabricate realities; electronic consumer; self-indulgent media
consumption; sixth childhood
Zodiac: Gemini II   *Tarot*: Devil
I Ching: Li (Light/Fire-Electricity)
Hebrew: Ayin ('my eyes fail for your salvation')
Titan: Theia

Stage 17   neuro-electric intelligence; control of one's own brain; the
sixth actualization; self-responsible reality fabrication; the
ego as neuro-computer programmer; creative use of
quantum electric media technologies; the age of neural
engineering; reality movies that you have scripted and
directed yourself
Zodiac: Cancer II   *Tarot*: Tower
I Ching: Li (Light/Fire-Electricity)
Hebrew: Pe ('the entrance of your words gives light')
Titan: Cronus

Stage 18   neuro-electric fusion; telepathy; telepathic linkage to genetic
consciousness; brain-fusing with other self-directed brains (i.e.
Gods); net communities; the sixth hive; high-orbital mini-earths;
the sixth migration
Zodiac: Leo II   *Tarot*: Star
I Ching: Li (Light/Fire-Electricity)
Hebrew: Tzad-Di ('I am consumed by insight; I work with
pure elements')   *Titan*: Hyperion

The sixth brain consists of the nervous system becoming aware of itself, apart from imprinted, gravitational reality-maps (Circuits 1–4) and even from body-rapture (Circuit 5). John Lilly calls this 'meta-programming', i.e. awareness of programming one's own programming. This Einsteinian, relativistic consciousness (conscious-intelligence) recognizes, for instance, that the Euclidian, Newtonian and Aristotelian reality-maps are three among billions of possible programs or models of experience. This level of brain functioning seems to have been reported first around 500 BC among various occult groups that were connected by the Silk Route (China–North India). It is so far beyond the terrestrial circuits that those who have achieved it can barely communicate about it to ordinary humanity (Circuits 1–4) and can hardly be understood even by fifth-circuit Rapture Engineers.

The characteristics of the neuroelectric circuit are high velocity, multiple choice, relativity, and the fission-fusion of all perceptions into parallel sci-fi universes of alternate possibilities. The mammalian politics that monitor power-struggles among terrestrial humanity are here transcended (i.e. seen as static, artificial and an elaborate façade). One is neither coercively manipulated into another's territorial reality nor forced to struggle against it with reciprocal, emotional game-playing (the usual soap-opera dramatics). One simply elects, consciously, whether or not to share the other's reality-model. Tactics for opening and imprinting the sixth circuit are described but rarely experienced in advanced raja-yoga, in the hermetic (coded) manuals of the medieval-Renaissance alchemists and illuminati.

No specific sixth-circuit chemical is yet available, but strong psychedelics like mescaline (from the 'sacred' cactus, peyote) psilocybin (from the Mexican 'magic mushroom', *teonactl*) and LSD open the nervous-system to a mixed-media series of Circuit 5 and Circuit 6 channels. This is appropriately called 'tripping', as distinguished from straightforward fifth-circuit 'turning on' or 'getting high'.

The suppression of scientific research in this area has had the unfortunate result of turning the outlaw drug-culture back toward fifth-circuit hedonics and pre-scientific tunnel-realities (in, for example, the occult revival, solipsism, and 'pop-orientalism'). Without scientific discipline and methodology, few can successfully decode the often-frightening (but philosophically crucial) sixth-circuit meta-programming signals. Such scientists as do continue to study this subject dare not publish their results (which are illegal) and record ever-wider tunnel-realities only in private conversations, as experienced by scholars in the era of the Inquisitorial. (Voltaire announced the Age of Reason two centuries too soon. We are still in the Dark Ages.) Most underground alchemists have given up on such challenging and risky self-work and restrict their trips to fifth-circuit erotic tunnels.

The evolutionary function of the sixth circuit is to enable us to communicate at Einsteinian relativities and neuro-electric accelerations, not using third-circuit laryngeal-manual symbols but directly via feedback, telepathy and computer link-up. Neuro-electric signals will increasingly replace 'speech' (hominid grunts) after space migration. When humans have climbed out of the atmosphere-gravity well of planetary life, accelerated sixth-circuit contellgence will make possible high-energy communication with 'Higher Intelligences', i.e., ourselves-in-the-future and other post-terrestrial races. It is charmingly simple and obvious, once we realize that the spaced-out neural experiences really are extraterrestrial, that getting high and spacing out are accurate metaphors. Circuit 5 neurosomatic rapture is preparation for the next step in our evolution, migration off the planet. Circuit 6 is preparation for the step after that: interspecies communication with advanced entities possessing electronic (post-verbal) tunnel-realities. Circuit 6 is the 'universal translator' often imagined by sci-fi writers. It is already built into our brains by the DNA tape, just as the circuits of the future butterfly are already built into the caterpillar.

CIRCUIT 7: **Neurogenetic Circuit: Decode And Redesign DNA Technology**
Ecological niche: DNA structure
Reality goal: control of DNA and egg-hive dynamics; genetic
self-reward; new species capable of manipulating and becoming
quantum-gravitational-field entities

Stage 19   neurogenetic passive-receptivity use of DNA technology;
self-definition as caste-bound hive member; self-indulgent
stage; genetic consumerism; gene-pool consciousness; sperm
intelligence; longevity; rejuvenation; awareness of influence of
genetics on individuation; age of genetic intelligence; seventh
childhood

Zodiac: Virgo II   *Tarot*: Moon
I Ching: Sun (Seed, blown by the wind)
Hebrew: Koph ('concerning your testimonies, I have
known of old you have founded them forever')
Titan: Phoebe

Stage 20   neurogenetic intelligence; the DNA mind; genetic engineering;
the seventh self-actualization; egg-wisdom; hive selection;
cloning; longevity and rejuvenation via DNA management; web-
film of life covering rock planet pushing up sperm-egg blossoms
to migrate into space; living inside spheres of one's own design,
enlivened by consciously co-operating web of species

Zodiac: Libra II   *Tarot*: Sun
I Ching: Sun (Seed, blown by the wind)
Hebrew: Resh ('knowledge is not for earthlings. Your plan
is eternal')   *Titan*: Mnemosyne

Stage 21   neurogenetic fusion; conscious symbiosis; self-actualized
genetic operatives begin to swarm and link up to create post-
biological entities; the seventh migration; formation of the
seventh hive; conscious recruitment of caste-elements to
fabricate new species

Zodiac: Scorpio II   *Tarot*: Judgement
I Ching: Sun (Seed, blown by the wind)
Hebrew: Shin ('I praise you in seven ways')
Titan: Crius

The seventh brain kicks into action when the nervous system begins to receive signals from within the individual neuron, from the DNA-RNA dialogue. The first to achieve this mutation spoke of 'memories of past lives', 'reincarnation', 'immortality', etc. That these adepts were recording something real is indicated by the fact that many of them (especially Hindus and Sufis) gave marvellously accurately poetic vistas of evolution 1,000 or 2,000 years before Darwin, and foresaw Superhumanity before Nietzsche. The 'akashic records' of Theosophy, the 'collective unconscious' of Jung, the 'phylogenetic unconscious' of Grof and Ring, are three modern metaphors for this circuit. The visions of past and future evolution described by those who have had 'out-of-body' experiences during close-to-death episodes also describes the trans-time Circuit 7 tunnel-reality. Specific exercises to trigger Circuit 7 are not to be found in yogic teaching; it usually happens, if at all, after several years of the kind of advanced raja-yoga that develops Circuit 6 facility.

The specific Circuit 7 neurotransmitter is, of course, LSD. (Peyote and psilocybin produce some Circuit 7 experiences also.) Circuit 7 is best considered, in terms of 1977 science, as the genetic archives, activated by anti-histone proteins, of DNA memory coiling back to the dawn of life. A sense of the inevitability of immortality and interspecies symbiosis comes to all Circuit 7 mutants. We now see that this, also, is an evolutionary forecast, since we stand right now on the doorstep of extended longevity, leading to immortality. The exact role of the right-lobe circuits and the reason for their activation in the 1960s cultural revolution now becomes clear. As sociologist F. M. Esfandiary writes in *Upwingers*, "Today when we speak of immortality and of going to another world we no longer mean these in a theological or metaphysical sense. People are now travelling to other worlds. People are now striving for immortality. Transcendence is no longer a metaphysical concept. It has become reality". The evolutionary function of the seventh circuit and its evolutionary, aeon-spanning tunnel-reality is to prepare us for conscious immortality and interspecies symbiosis.

CIRCUIT 8: **Neuro-Atomic/Metaphysiological Circuit (Post-Biological)**

Ecological niche: atomic and gravitational fields
Individual evolutionary level: (highly speculative) probably post-biological life as information patterns
Reality goal: fusion into black hole (?)

Stage 22

meta-physiological neuro-atomic consciousness; self-definition as atomic consciousness; quantum consumer; imprinting the nervous-system and DNA by electro-gravitational force-field structures and nuclear particles; awareness and manipulation of sub-atomic nuclear energy by the nervous system; self-indulgent use of quantum reality and nanotechnology in post-gravitational environment; eighth childhood

Zodiac: Sagittarius II	*Tarot*: (no card)
I Ching: Chien (Heaven)	
Hebrew: (no letter)	*Titan*: Coeus

Stage 23

meta-physiological/neuro-atomic intelligence; the galactic central computer; eighth self-actualization; executive management of Schwarzschild Radius energies; mastery of nuclear and gravitational energies; star-making via controlled nuclear fusion; the age when nuclear fusion combined with gravitational mechanics makes possible post-terrestrial travel

Zodiac: Capricorn II	*Tarot*: Universe
I Ching: Chien (Heaven)	
Hebrew: ('let my soul live')	*Titan*: Lapetus

Stage 24

meta-physiological fusion in black hole; creation of new hives (e.g. new big bang?); new astronomical forms; galactic domesticity; the ulti-mate re-union of the attractives; the absorption of matter (i.e. frozen information) into the Violet Whole; the in-tegration of your evolving in-formation with those of other singularities; the final migration of the cycle

Zodiac: Aquarius II	*Tarot*: (no card)
I Ching: Chien (Heaven)	
Hebrew: (no letter)	*Titan*: Themis

Hold on to your hats and breathe deeply: this is the farthest out that human intelligence has yet ventured. Consciousness probably precedes the biological unit or DNA tape-loop. 'Out-of-body experiences', 'astral projection', contact with alien (extra-terrestrial?) 'entities' or with a galactic Overmind, etc., such as I've experienced, have all been reported for thousands of years, not merely by the ignorant, the superstitious or the gullible, but often by the finest minds among us.[20]

Circuit 8 is neuro-atomic—or infra, supra and meta-physiological—being a quantum model of consciousness and/or a conscious model of quantum mechanics.[21] When the nervous system is turned on to this quantum-level circuit, space-time is obliterated. Einstein's speed-of-light barrier is transcended; in Dr. Sarfatti's metaphor, we escape 'electromagnetic chauvinism'. The contellignence within the quantum projection booth *is* the entire cosmic 'brain', just as the micro-miniaturized DNA helix *is* the local brain guiding planetary evolution. As Lao-tse said from his own Circuit 8 perspective, "The greatest is within the smallest". Circuit 8 is triggered by Ketamine, a neuro-chemical researched by Dr. John Lilly, which is also (according to a wide-spread but unconfirmed rumour) given to astronauts to prepare them for space. High doses of LSD also produce some Circuit 8 quantum awareness.

This neuro-atomic contellignence is four mutations beyond terrestrial domesticity. (The current ideological struggle is between Circuit 4 tribal moralists-or-collectivists and Circuit 5 hedonic individualists.) When our need for higher intelligence, or for richer involvement in the cosmic script, further transcendence will no longer be satisfied by physical bodies, not even by immortal bodies hopping across space-time at warp 9; Circuit 8 will open a further frontier to new universes and realities: "beyond theology: the science and art of Godmanship", as Alan Watts once wrote. It is therefore possible that the mysterious 'entities', angels and extraterrestrials monotonously reported by Circuit 8 visionaries are members or races already evolved to this level. But it is also possible, as Leary and Sarfatti more recently suggest, that They are ourselves-in-the-future.

The left-lobe terrestrial circuits contain the learned lessons of our evolutionary past (and present). The right-lobe extraterrestrial circuits are the evolutionary script for out future. Thus far, there have been two alternative explanations of why the Drug

---

20. Such experiences are reported daily to parapsychologists and have been experienced by scientists such scientists as Dr. John Lilly. Dr. Kenneth Ring has attributed these phenomena to what he calls, very appropriately, 'the extraterrestrial unconscious'.

21. As suggested by turned-on physicists, such as John Archibald-Wheeler, Saul Paul Sirag, Dr. Fritjof Capra, and Jack Sarfatti. It is suggested that the 'atomic consciousness' first proposed by Leary in *The Seven Tongues of God* (1962) is the explanatory link which will unite parapsychology and paraphysics into the first scientific empirical experimental theology in history.

Revolution happened. The first is presented in a sophisticated way by anthropologist Weston LaBarre, and in an ignorant, moralistic way by most anti-drug propaganda in the schools and mass media. This explanation says, in essence, that millions have turned away from the legal *down* drugs to illegal *high* drugs because we are living in troubled times and many are seeking escape into fantasy. This theory, at its best, only partially explains the ugliest and most publicized aspect of the revolution: the reckless drug-abuse characteristic of the immature. It says nothing about the millions of respectable doctors, lawyers, engineers, etc., who have turned away from second-circuit intoxication with booze to fifth-circuit rapture with weed. Nor does it account at all for the thoughtful, philosophical sixth-circuit investigations of persons of high intelligence and deep sensibility, such as Aldous Huxley, Stan Grof, Masters and Houston, Alan W. Watts, Carlos Castaneda, John Lilly and thousands of scientific and lay researchers on consciousness.

A more plausible theory, devised by psychiatrist Norman Zinberg, out of the work of Marshall McLuhan, holds that modern electronic media have so shifted the nervous-system's parameters that young people no longer enjoy 'linear' drugs like alcohol and find meaning only in 'non-linear' weed and psychedelics. This is certainly part of the truth, but it is too narrow and overstresses TV and computers without sufficiently stressing the general technological picture: the ongoing science-fiction revolution, of which the most significant aspects are Space Migration, Increased Intelligence and Life Extension, which Leary has condensed into his $S.M.I^2.L.E.$ formula. Space Migration plus Increased Intelligence plus Life Extension means expansion of humanity into all space-time. $S.M. + I^2. + L.E. = \text{infinity}$.

Without totally endorsing Charles Fort's technological mysticism ("It steam-engines when it comes steam-engine time"), it is obvious that the DNA metaprogram for planetary evolution is far wiser than any of our individual nervous systems, which are, in a sense, giant robots or sensors for DNA. Early science-fiction of brilliant writers like Stapledon, Clarke, Heinlein; Kubrick's 2001; all were increasingly clear DNA signals transmitted through the intuitive right lobe of sensitive artists, preparing us for the extraterrestrial mutation.

It is scarcely coincidental that mainstream 'literary' intellectuals—the heir of the Platonic-aristocratic tradition that a gentleman never uses his hands, monkeys with tools or learns a manual craft—despise both science fiction and the dope culture. Nor is it coincidental that the *Whole Earth Catalogs*—created by Stewart Brand, a graduate of Ken Kesey's Merry Pranksters--are the New Testament of the rural drop-out culture, each issue bulging with tons of eco-technological information about all the manual, dextrous, gadgety know-how that Plato and his heirs consider fit only for slaves. Not surprisingly, Brand's latest publication, *Co-Evolution Quarterly*, has been devoted to publicizing Prof. Gerard O'Neill's space-habitat, L5. Nor is it an accident that dopers seem to prefer science-fiction to any other reading, even including the extraterrestrial-flavoured Hindu scriptures and occult-shamanic Circuit 6-7 trip-poets like Crowley and Hesse. The Circuit 6 drugs may have contributed much to the metaprogramming consciousness that has led to sudden awareness of 'male chauvinism' (women's liberationists), 'species chauvinism' (ecology, Lilly's dolphin studies), 'type-G star chauvinism' (Carl Sagan), and even 'oxygen chauvinism' (the CETI conference), etc. The imprinted tunnel-realities which identify one as 'white-male-American-earthian' etc. or 'black-female-Cuban' etc. are no longer big enough to enclose our exploding contelligence.

As *Time* magazine reported on November 26, 1973, "Within ten years, according to pharmacologists, they will have perfected pills and cranial electrodes for providing life-long bliss for everyone on Earth". The 1960s hysteria about weed and acid was just the overture to this fifth-circuit break-through. Nathan S. Kline, M.D., predicts real aphrodisiacs, drugs to speed up learning, and drugs to foster or terminate any behaviour. There were those who were burnt or jailed at the beginning of the Revolution of Outer Technology; and those who were jailed or beaten by cops in the 1960s, who were forerunners of the Revolution of Inner Technology. *Star Trek* is a better guide to the emerging reality than anything in the *New York Review of Books*. In short, the various levels of consciousness and circuits we have been discussing, and illustrating, are all biochemical imprints in the evolution of the nervous system. Each imprint creates a bigger tunnel-reality. In the Sufi metaphor, the donkey on which we ride becomes a different donkey after each imprint. The metaprogrammer continually learns more and is increasingly able to be aware of itself operating. We are thus evolving to intelligence-studying-intelligence (the nervous system studying the nervous system) and are more and more capable of accelerating our own evolution. Leary now symbolizes intelligence-studying-intelligence by the mark, I^2. On the lower levels, you see with one 'I', so to speak. On the higher levels, you see with many 'I's. And space-time shifts from three Euclidean dimensions to non-Euclidean multi-dimensionality.